The Nature Kid's Guide to
JELLYFISH

DAVID ANDERSON

LP Media Inc. Publishing
Text copyright © 2026 by LP Media Inc.
All rights reserved.

For information address LP Media Inc. Publishing,
30012 Variolite St NW, Princeton MN 55371
www.lpmedia.org

Publication Data

Jellyfish
The Nature Kid's Guide to Jellyfish — First edition.

Summary: "Learn all about Jellyfish, the Nature Kid Way"
— Provided by publisher.

ISBN: 979-8-89818-212-0

[1. Jellyfish – Non-Fiction] I. Title.

Title: The Nature Kid's Guide to Jellyfish

CONTENTS

JELLYFISH MYSTERIES

A big group of jellyfish swimming together is called a smack!

Whoosh! A jellyfish drifts through the dark ocean.

Even though they have "fish" in their name, jellyfish are not really fish at all. They have no bones, no blood, and no brain. Their bodies are soft and squishy, kind of like jelly! That's how they got their name.

These animals have lived in the ocean for over 500 million years. That means they were here long before the dinosaurs!

Jellyfish float and drift with the waves. Some are tiny as a grain of rice. Others stretch wider than a car. You can find them in every ocean on Earth, from icy polar waters to warm tropical seas.

BRAINLESS BRILLIANCE

A jellyfish is about 95 percent water — even more watery than a cucumber!

Bloop! A jellyfish pulses its bell and glides ahead.

A jellyfish body is like a soft bag of water. The top part is called a **bell**. It opens and closes to push the jelly along, kind of like squeezing a water balloon.

Long arms called **tentacles** hang below the bell. Jellyfish use them to catch food and defend themselves.

A jellyfish has only one opening in its body. That same hole is used for eating food and getting rid of waste. So a jellyfish's mouth and its stomach exit are the exact same spot. It sounds gross, but it works for the jellyfish!

STINGING SECRETS

A single jellyfish tentacle can hold thousands of tiny stingers ready to fire!

Zap! A jellyfish cruises along, its tentacles dragging behind.

Jellyfish tentacles are covered in thousands of tiny sting cells, each one coiled up tight like a spring. When something brushes against a tentacle, pop! The stinger fires faster than a bullet.

The sting shoots **venom** into the other animal. Venom is like a poison. It can stun small fish so the jelly can eat them.

Most jellyfish stings just hurt a little bit. But some are very strong and dangerous. It is smart to stay away from all jellyfish in the wild.

GLOWING JELLIES

Flash! A deep sea jelly lights up the pitch-dark water.

Some jellyfish can make their own light. This is called **bioluminescence**. It happens deep in the ocean where sunlight never reaches.

These jellies glow in blue, green, or purple. The light comes from a special chemical mix inside their body. No batteries needed!

Glowing can scare off hunters or confuse them. It can also call for help from bigger animals nearby. In the deep sea, light is a powerful survival tool.

Some jellyfish flash their glow on and off like a living alarm system!

MOON MYSTERIES

Moon jellyfish sometimes wash up on beaches by the hundreds after a storm!

Swish! A pale moon jelly floats near the sandy shore.

Moon jellyfish are one of the most common jellies in the world. They are clear with a soft pink or purple glow. Look closely at the top. You can see four rings shaped like horseshoes. Those are their stomachs!

These jellies live in warm and cool waters all around the world. They like to stay close to the coast where food is plentiful.

Moon jellies eat tiny bits of food that float in the water. They use their short tentacles to grab meals as they drift along with the current.

DEADLY VISION

A box jellyfish has 24 eyes spread around its cube-shaped bell!

Zoom! A box jelly speeds through warm tropical water.

Box jellyfish have a square-shaped bell. That is how they got their name. Unlike most jellies that just drift, box jellies are fast swimmers. They can steer exactly where they want to go.

These jellies have real eyes that can see light and shapes. Most jellyfish just float around blindly, but box jellies can actually hunt their prey.

Box jellyfish live in warm ocean waters near Australia and Asia. Their sting is one of the strongest in the animal kingdom. Swimmers must be very careful around them.

MANE MONSTER

The lion's mane jellyfish can have more than 800 tentacles at once!

Swoosh! Long red tentacles trail through icy water.

The lion's mane jellyfish is the biggest jelly in the sea. Its bell can grow over 6 feet wide, bigger than a car! Its tentacles can stretch more than 100 feet long!

This giant jelly lives in cold northern waters near Alaska, Canada, and Europe. It swims near the top of the sea where it catches small fish and shrimp.

The lion's mane has thick, flowing tentacles that look like a lion's shaggy hair. That is how this ocean giant got its fierce name.

MAN O' WAR

FUN
FACT!

A man o' war's tentacles can grow to 100 feet long — longer than a basketball court!

Pop! A bright blue bubble bobs on top of the warm waves.

The Portuguese man o' war looks like a jellyfish, but it is not one. It is actually a **colony**. That means it is made of many tiny animals working together as a team.

The top part is a blue or purple gas bag filled with air. It floats on the water like a sail. Wind pushes it across the ocean wherever the breeze blows.

Long tentacles hang below, trailing through the water. They can sting very hard. Even when a man o' war washes up dead on shore, those tentacles can still sting for days.

FOREVER JELLYFISH

Immortal jellyfish travel the world by hitching rides on the bottom of ships!

Poof! An old jelly shrinks and starts its life again.

Most animals grow old and die. But the immortal jellyfish has an amazing secret trick. When it gets sick or old, it can turn back into a baby and start over!

This tiny jelly is smaller than a pinky nail, only about 4 millimeters wide. It lives in warm oceans around the world.

Scientists study this jelly to learn how it resets its body. No other animal can do this in quite the same way. It is like having a restart button for life.

ALARM ATOLLA

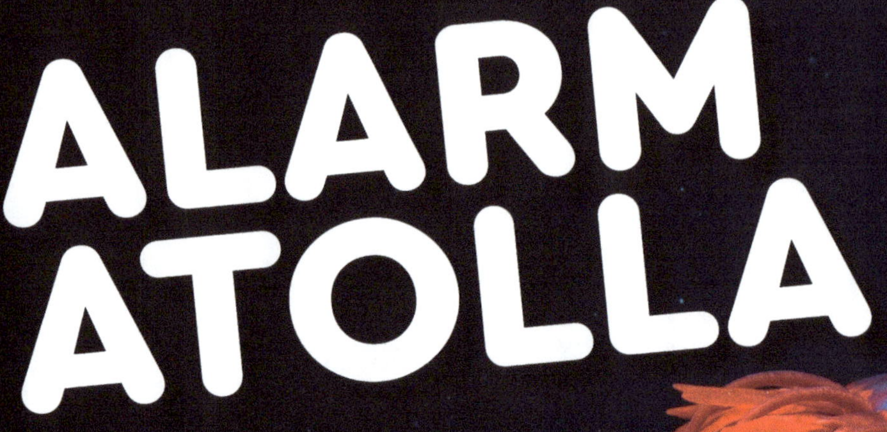

Scientists nicknamed the atolla the 'alarm jellyfish' because of its flashing light trick!

Whirl! A deep sea jelly spins and flashes bright blue.

The atolla jellyfish lives deep in the ocean, nearly a mile below the surface. It is dark red with a round, flat bell. Most animals cannot see it down in the darkness.

When a big animal attacks, the atolla has a clever plan. It makes a spinning ring of bright blue light. This light show works like a burglar alarm!

The flashing light draws even bigger animals to the scene. They come and scare the attacker away. Meanwhile, the atolla escapes into the darkness.

EGG JELLIES

DID YOU KNOW?
The fried egg jellyfish can grow wider than a dinner plate — up to 16 inches across!

Splat! A jelly that looks just like a fried egg drifts by.

The fried egg jellyfish really does look like breakfast. It has a round white bell with a bright yellow blob in the middle. Sunny side up!

This jelly floats in warm seas around the Mediterranean. It moves slowly and calmly through the water. Small crabs sometimes ride on top of its bell for a free trip across the ocean!

Fried egg jellies have a mild sting that barely hurts. They eat tiny animals and even smaller jellies that float nearby.

TINY TERROR

Swimmers in Australia wear special full-body suits to protect from irukandji stings!

Zing! A jelly smaller than a grape gives a big sting.

The irukandji jellyfish is one of the smallest and most dangerous jellies in the world. It is about the size of a fingertip. Its bell is almost completely clear, making it nearly invisible in the water.

This little jelly lives in warm waters near Australia. Unlike most jellies, it can sting with both its tentacles and its bell.

Its sting can make a person very sick for days. Swimmers learn to watch out for it even though it is so tiny. Sometimes the smallest things pack the biggest punch.

BARREL BUDDIES

Barrel jellyfish have no long tentacles — just eight frilly mouth arms for catching food!

Bump! A huge jelly rolls in with the ocean's tide.

Barrel jellyfish are big and round like a barrel. They are one of the largest jellies that swim near land. Some can weigh up to 75 pounds, as heavy as a big dog!

These jellies live in waters around Europe and the British Isles. They often wash up on beaches in summer. Their sting is gentle and mostly harmless to people.

Sea turtles love to munch on barrel jellies. To a hungry turtle, these soft, squishy jellyfish make a perfect meal.

CRIMSON COMB

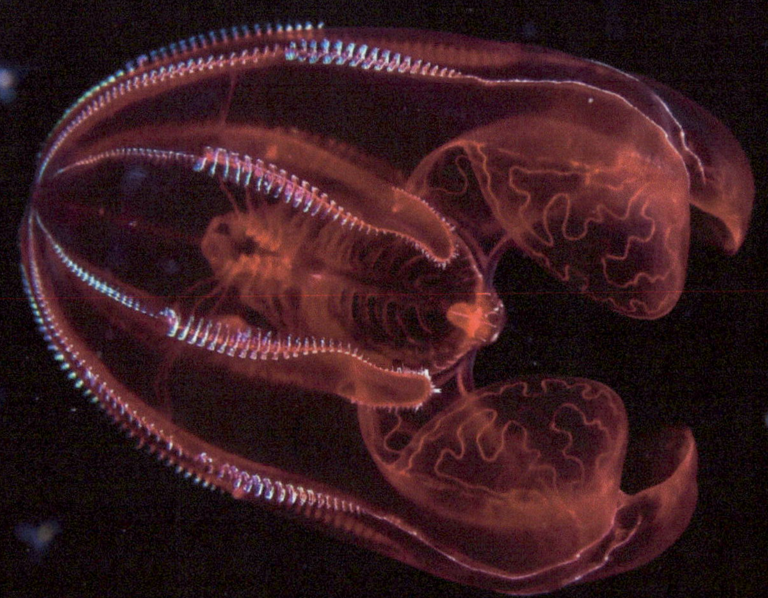

Comb jellies have been on Earth even longer than true jellyfish — over 700 million years!

Shimmer! A blood-red jelly gleams in the deep, dark sea.

The bloodybelly comb jelly has a deep red belly that helps it hide. Down in the dark ocean, red looks black. Hunters swim right past without spotting it.

This jelly is not a true jellyfish at all. It belongs to a group called comb jellies. Tiny rows of combs line its body and help it swim. When light hits the combs, they shimmer with rainbow colors.

Comb jellies do not sting like true jellyfish. Instead, they catch food with sticky cells that trap tiny prey.

SOLAR SWIMMERS

In Jellyfish Lake in Palau, millions of golden jellies migrate across the lake every day!

Swirl! Spotted jellies follow the sun across a warm lagoon.

Spotted lagoon jellyfish are covered in white polka dots. They live in warm lagoons and shallow bays. Every single day, these jellies swim toward the sunlight.

Why do they chase the sun? Tiny plants called algae live inside their body. The algae need sunlight to make food, and they share that food with the jelly. Both partners help each other survive.

Spotted lagoon jellies have a very mild sting. Most people cannot even feel it when they touch one.

GLOWING GHOST

The crystal jelly's glowing protein helped scientists win a Nobel Prize in 2008!

34

Glow! A see-through jelly lights up with green fire.

The crystal jellyfish is almost invisible. Its body is clear like glass, with over 100 delicate tentacles trailing behind. But when something touches it, the jelly glows a bright green color.

This jelly lives along the west coast of North America, from Alaska to California. It floats near the surface in calm waters.

Scientists love to study this jelly. The chemical that makes it glow helped them invent new ways to look at tiny living things inside the body. One little jellyfish changed science forever.

JELLYFISH TAKEOVER

DID YOU KNOW?

In 2009, a massive bloom of giant jellyfish in Japan actually tipped over a fishing boat!

Swarm! Thousands of jellies fill a warm, crowded bay.

The ocean is getting warmer. More jellyfish are showing up in many places around the world. When too many jellies fill the water at once, it is called a bloom.

Blooms can happen when the water gets too warm or too polluted. Fish that normally eat jellies are disappearing, so jelly numbers keep growing and growing.

People are working hard to keep the oceans clean and healthy. A balanced ocean needs the right mix of fish, jellyfish, and other sea life.

JELLYFISH JUBILEE

Some aquariums have special jellyfish rooms with rainbow lights that make the jellies glow!

Pulse! A graceful jelly dances through a sunlit sea.

Jellyfish are some of the most amazing animals on Earth. They glow, sting, drift, and dance through the waves. Each kind has its own special way of living in the sea.

We can help jellyfish by keeping the ocean clean. Picking up trash and using less plastic makes a big difference for all ocean animals.

Next time you see a jellyfish, take a close look. These creatures have no brain, no heart, and no bones. Yet they have survived for millions of years. They have so much to teach us about life in the sea.

GLOSSARY

bell

The dome-shaped top part of a jellyfish body

tentacles

Long, thin arms that hang below a jellyfish

venom

A poison some animals use to sting

bioluminescence

Light made by a living thing's own body

colony

Many tiny animals living and working together as one